First Edition published September 2017.

ISBN-13: 978-0-9904973-2-5
ISBN-10: 0990497321

White Horse LDS Books
Salt Lake City, Utah

www.myldsbooks.com

Cover Design by Connie & Stephen Gorton

THREE MINUTES EIGHTEEN SECONDS

A PROPHET'S MESSAGE TO THE WORLD (AND TO YOU)

BY BILL WYLSON

Author's Note: The principles discussed in this work relate to doctrines, procedures and practices of The Church of Jesus Christ of Latter-day Saints. I have attempted to cite sources from the scriptures and from the published writings of the General Authorities of the Church. Nevertheless, I have no authority or commission to speak in any official capacity for the Church. The ideas expressed herein represent nothing more than the opinion of the author.

TABLE OF CONTENTS

"Since the world began, God has raised up prophets who speak the will of heaven to the people of their times. It is our responsibility to listen and then apply the messages the Lord provides for us."

- Dieter F. Uchtdorf

Imagine for a minute that you receive a phone call from President Monson's secretary informing you that the prophet would like to meet with you at his office. President Monson has requested a moment of your time because he has something important to tell you. Would you be curious to hear what the prophet wants to say to you? Would you be filled with wonder? Concern? Excitement? Anticipation? Would you consider that his message for you might be extremely significant, perhaps even critical?

THE POWER OF WORDS

> *"How sweet are thy words unto my taste! yea, sweeter than honey to my mouth!"*
>
> *- Psalms 119:103*

I love words. Words are extremely powerful.

Describing the power of words, Lord Byron poetically portrays this truth:

> *"But words are things, and a small drop of ink,*
> *Falling like dew, upon a thought, produces*
> *That which makes thousands, perhaps*
> *millions, think."*

The power of words can make thousands, even millions, stop and think. I would like you to take a few minutes to *think* about the power of words.

"Have you ever stopped to consider the power of words?" asks Randall Wright. *"Through mere words, wars have started and ended. Tender feelings have been hurt and soothed. Courage has been instilled and fear has been implanted. Lives have been destroyed and others changed for the better. Think back on your own life when words have hurt you deeply or have comforted and given you strength and hope to do better"*

A single word can inspire and brighten your entire day. Conversely, a single word can drag you into the depths of despair and gloom. Words can be used to create and uplift; words can be used to tear down and destroy.

Joyce Meyer has described words as containers. Containers for what? As she explains, words are containers for power.

"Words are containers for power. You choose what kind of power they carry."

- Joyce Meyer

More specifically, Charles Capps stated: *"Words are the most powerful thing in the universe.... Words are containers. They contain faith, or fear, and they produce after their kind."* [1]

The artful words of a beautifully crafted poem can impassion and motivate. The lyrical words of an uplifting song can evoke emotions of ardor, excitement, delight and joy. The sacred words of Holy Scripture can change hearts and lives.

Proverbs teaches us that: *"The tongue has the power of life and death."* [2]

At the last day, we shall even be judged *"according to the words which are written."*

"Wherefore, he shall bring forth his words unto them, which words shall judge them at the last day...

"Wherefore, these things shall go from generation to generation as long as the earth shall stand; and they shall go according to the will and pleasure of God; and the nations who shall possess them shall be judged of them according to the words which are written." [3]

Yes, words can be very powerful.

---

[1] Capps, Charles. From *The Tongue: A Creative Force*.
[2] Proverbs 18:21.
[3] 2 Nephi 25:18, 22.

In the ultimate sense, God spoke (words) and the worlds were created.

"For behold, by the power of his word man came upon the face of the earth, which earth was created by the power of his word." [4]

---

[4] Jacob 4:9.

THREE COMPELLING WORDS

> *"Gentle words, quiet words, are after all the most powerful words. They are more convincing, more compelling, more prevailing."*
>
> - *Washington Gladden*

I would like to examine three *"small drops of ink"*, as Lord Byron calls them, that are, simultaneously, extremely powerful words.

The first word I would like you to consider is the word "Critical."

What feelings do you associate with the word critical? Does the word produce any intense emotions for you? Is it a container for faith or for fear? What makes this specific word so powerful?

According to the dictionary definition, critical means:

"Expressing adverse or disapproving comments of judgment."

You could, for example, be critical of your spouse's driving or critical of the way your teenager keeps his bedroom. These are, perhaps, stressful situations but not likely deeply emotional.

A second definition of the word critical is:

"To express an analysis of the merits and faults of a work of art, music or literature."

This meaning suggests the way we might be critical of a painting we don't like, or of an annoying piece of music, or of poetry that fails to move us emotionally. It speaks more of a clinical, perhaps even mechanical, response rather than a powerfully penetrating reaction.

The third definition of critical, and the one I want to emphasize as a formidable expression thick with emotion, is:

"Having the potential to become disastrous; at a point of crisis."

If your boss tells you, *"It's critical that you have these papers done by morning,"* it might necessitate you staying late at the office or possibly taking work home with you. No doubt that would be inconvenient and could, perhaps, stir some emotions of resentment or even anger toward your unreasonable employer, but certainly it wouldn't be (or shouldn't be, anyway) powerful enough to evoke emotions that upend your life.

Now imagine that your spouse tells you she (or he) isn't feeling well. Being concerned for her health and well-being, you drive her to the emergency room at your local hospital. You worriedly wait while the doctors run tests, anxious for word about her condition. Unexpectedly, you overhear the doctor notifying a nurse, *"Her condition is critical."*

What emotions are arising in you now? Ask yourself again, what feelings do you associate with the word critical? Does the word produce any intense emotions for you?

Can you sense how powerful the word critical can be?

"A word after a word after a word is power."

- Margaret Atwood

The next word and second *"small drop of ink"* I'd ask you to contemplate is the word "essential." How stirring is the word essential?

As an adjective, essential means *"absolutely necessary; extremely important."*

What significant emotions do you attach to the word essential? Consider how essential it is that your tax forms be mailed to the IRS by April 15th. If you have a job, is it essential that your time cards are filled out properly and on time?

Tax Day definitely generates intense emotions for some...panic, relief, dismay. Not filling out a time card could create feelings of disappointment and frustration when you discover that your paycheck is delayed.

Imagine now that you decide to hike a scenic mountain trail. As you painstakingly climb the steep terrain you stop to rest on a sun baked stone next to the trail, not noticing the rattlesnake cooling itself in the shade beside the rock. The rattler, thinking that you intend to harm it, lunges at you, biting you in the leg. The snake silently slithers away, leaving you to wonder, *"What am I going to do now?"*

With a look of terror in your eyes you turn to your hiking partner as he reaches for the hunting knife he has sheathed on his belt. Your leg writhes in pain as you watch the sharp knife blade gleaming in the sunlight. Your partner exclaims, *"It's essential that we get the poison out of your blood stream."*

Now what intense emotions do you affix to that specific use of the word essential? How stirring is the word essential in that context?

Finally, the third word I'd like you to mull over is the word "vital."

The dictionary tells us that vital means *"absolutely necessary or important; essential."* This first definition is similar to the meaning of the word essential. For instance, we think of water as being vital or essential to sustaining life.

The second definition of vital is *"full of energy, lively."* How does this characterization of the word affect you? What feelings does the word vital arouse?

Envision yourself walking down a peaceful suburban street. Unexpectedly you come upon a man lying motionless on the ground. You cautiously approach the prone figure. He seems unresponsive and appears not to be breathing. You check for a pulse and find none. As you prepare to begin CPR you call 911. The Emergency Dispatcher on the other end of the phone asks for the man's condition and you respond, *"I'm not getting any vital signs!"*

You realize in desperation that it is vital (absolutely necessary or essential) that you restore this man's vitality (energy, liveliness). The word vital suddenly becomes a matter of life and death.

In certain settings and circumstances, the words critical, essential and vital can become extremely powerful and significant. But what is it about these three compelling words that warrant a chapter in this book? You are about to find out.

A 3 ½ MINUTE INTERVIEW

"God loves us enough to send us prophets... we need to love Him enough to follow them."

- Sheldon F. Childs

Have you heard the expression *"an audience with the Pope?"* I have often wondered what it would take to be granted an audience with the Pope. Papal audiences are generally held on Wednesdays when and if the Pope is in Rome, giving visitors a distinctive opportunity to see the Pope and to obtain a Papal or apostolic blessing from the Pontiff.

23

The Pope offers a greeting in the language of the visiting group and may present lessons and instructions. After the assemblage, the Pope will offer the *"our Father"* prayer in Latin and impart his Apostolic Blessing upon the crowd.

A private audience with the Pontiff is significantly different and exceptional.

Tens of thousands of people would love a private audience with the Pope but that would be almost impossible without high level connections. A private audience with the Pope normally requires a letter of introduction from one's bishop and the acceptance of the invitation by the Pope or a member of his staff.

One couple wrote of their singular experience in obtaining an audience with Pope John Paul II.

> *"In 1992, we traveled with a group of 48 who were led by a monsignor who had close connections to then Pope John Paul II. Each couple had to make a substantial contribution/donation that was presented to the Pope during our private audience. We were on call from the time we arrived in Rome on a Monday until we finally received word to meet with the Pope on Friday. It was understood at the onset of the trip there was no guarantee we were going to actually have the private meeting*

based on the health and schedule of the Pope at that time.

"When we finally were granted the meeting, it was a once in a lifetime, awe inspiring audience with Pope John Paul II. We went up single file and could greet the Pope and then kiss his ring. He was quite elderly at the time but had a childlike aura about him. It is something I will never forget."

When I was a young boy growing up in Ohio, Elders Gordon B. Hinckley and Thomas S. Monson, General Authorities of the Church at that time, visited our home. The purpose of their visit was to call my father to serve as a Mission President. Even as a boy, I understood that these were important men, yet their humility and their humanity were fully evident.

Decades later, as prophet of the Church, President Gordon B. Hinckley issued a call to my father to serve as a Sealer in the Bountiful Temple. Our entire family was invited to meet with President Hinckley in his office in Salt Lake City where he presented the call. Not knowing beforehand the reason for the meeting, we were filled with anticipation and excitement. President Hinckley greeted each of us, then recollected his original visit to our home in Ohio before extending the calling. This was a solemn and sacred experience and one that left an indelible impression on my mind.

I still remember the day my father called me on the phone to inform me that the prophet had requested to visit with him and had invited the family to attend. I recall feeling thrilled and apprehensive at the same time and I wasn't even the one being called to serve.

What do you envision your reaction would be if you were granted an audience with a prophet of God?

Imagine for a minute if you will that you receive a phone call from President Monson's secretary informing you that the prophet would like to meet with you in his office. President Monson has requested a moment of your time because he has something important to tell you. Would you be curious to hear what the prophet wants to say to you? Would you be filled with wonder? Concern? Excitement? Anticipation? Would you consider that his message for you might be extremely significant, perhaps even *critical*?

The prophet's secretary then asks if you would be available Tuesday evening at 7 p.m., adding that the meeting should only take about three or four minutes of your time. Do you think you could clear your calendar for an audience with the prophet? I believe that most of the faithful members of the Church would do whatever it takes to be at that interview.

Now imagine further that you arrive at your meeting and, after the greeting and formalities are dispensed with, you are invited to take a seat in a chair across from President Monson. The room is filled with a spirit of peace and yet you still feel noticeably nervous. There is kindness and humility in the prophet's demeanor as he addresses you and yet you seem to detect an expression of concern in his voice as he leans forward and, in all earnestness and solemnity, instructs you in something that is critical for you to be doing. Yes, he actually uses that very powerful word *critical* and you sense the magnitude and gravity of his words. How much importance would you place on the words this man as the prophet of God is sharing with you?

> *"You need the strength that comes from trusting the Lord's prophets."*
>
> *- Neil L. Anderson*

In your approximately 3 ½ minute imaginary interview with President Monson you can sense the sincerity of his message and you begin to comprehend the concern he feels for you as he mentions something that is *essential* for you to obtain and maintain *vital* and alive. Would you take what the prophet said casually or would you immediately begin the process to obtain this essential element in your life?

As your interview ends and you leave President Monson's office, you step out of the building onto the busy streets of Salt Lake City, the words of the prophet still vibrant in your mind and in your heart. You ponder the critical call you have been issued and the essential aspect of character you have been asked to obtain and maintain vital and alive. What do you do next?

Do you tell yourself; "Wow, I really felt the Spirit during that interview. That was so uplifting and inspiring!" and then go on with your life as before? Do you tell yourself that you should probably think about making some changes in your life and maybe consider trying to do some of what the prophet advised you or do you do whatever it takes within your power to ensure that the critical, essential and vital aspects of the prophet's message become a critical, essential and vital component of your day-to-day existence?

Now imagine that your interview with President Monson, your audience with a prophet of God, wasn't imaginary at all. Because it wasn't.

A MESSAGE TO YOU (AND TO THE WORLD)

> *"If you will open your heart and listen to the words of the prophets, you can come to know, for yourself, what they teach is true."*
>
> *- Andrew (JustAnAverageMormon.org)*

During the Sunday morning session of the April 2017 General Conference, seven Church leaders addressed the world. The average length of each discourse was approximately 14 minutes, with the shortest talk taking just over 11 minutes and the longest lasting almost 19 minutes. The one exception in that morning's line-up of speakers was President Thomas S. Monson. President Monson stood and, due to health concerns, spoke to the world for only 3 minutes and 18 seconds. With little time and modest strength, the prophet of God conveyed a commanding and formidable message to the world and, through the power of the Holy Spirit, to you and me individually.

Knowing that he would have only a few moments to speak to us, do you suppose that President Monson considered carefully and chose prayerfully what declaration and testimonial he should impart to us? Do you imagine that the prophet, in those brief moments we were privileged to share an audience with him, felt deeply the words which he wanted us to hear from him? I was impressed that he chose three especially powerful and compelling words in delivering his brief but significant message to the world. I am certain you know by now the three words I am referring to.

After offering a warm greeting and prior to his formal message, President Monson announced the building of five new temples. This brief announcement in and of itself is a significant fulfillment of prophecy. The prophet Joseph Smith affirmed that *"we need the temple more than anything else."* [5]

---

[5] Smith, Joseph, *Journal History of the Church*, May 4, 1844.

We are a generation of temple builders, commanded by the Lord to build temples unto his holy name. [6] In obedience to this commandment, more and more temples to the Lord are being built throughout the world and, in many cases, under increasing and intense opposition. We can expect that the expansion of temple building will continue and increase as the church continues to grow. Brigham Young saw a time during the Millennium when thousands of temples would dot the earth and tens of thousands of faithful saints would enter and perform sacred ordinances there.

The Old Testament affirms that *"the Lord, whom ye seek, shall suddenly come to his temple."* [7] The Doctrine and Covenants attests: *"I am Jesus Christ, the Son of God; wherefore, gird up your loins and I will suddenly come to my temple."* [8]

---

[6] See D&C 124:39.
[7] Malachi 3:1.
[8] D&C 36:8.

Critical

Following the announcement of five new temples, President Monson began his formal message, stating: *"I speak about the power of the Book of Mormon and the critical need we have as members of this Church to study, ponder, and apply its teachings in our lives."* The necessity of reading, studying and pondering the teachings of the Book of Mormon and then applying its principles and instructions in our lives is critical. *"The importance of having a firm and sure testimony of the Book of Mormon,"* continued President Monson, *"cannot be overstated."*

Hugh Nibley has emphasized that:

> *"In reading the Book of Mormon no one is ever doing something he shouldn't be doing. Most of the time he would be doing probably the best thing he could possibly be doing. If it is not itself the best thing to be doing, it will quickly put you onto the best thing to be doing because it will have a direct effect on you. It will change you; it will work on you. It is a personal, intimate document. It will hit you. You can't just read the Book of Mormon and nothing else. It immediately puts you on the high road to what you should be doing, like no other book. And it will lead you directly into a course of thought or*

a course of action of the greatest significance to yourself and to the world you live in." [9]

The Book of Mormon illustrates the power of words in drawing hearts and souls to the Savior. Its mission is to bring us to Christ. Inspired authors were aware that this critical mission would take place through the words which they were writing. Nephi explains that *"the words of the faithful should speak as if it were from the dead."* [10]

"The words and phrases of the Book of Mormon are 'powerful and great.' Treasures await the pondering mind that contemplates virtually every word, idiom, figure of speech, or semantic value in the texts of this remarkable record."

- John Welch

---

[9] Nibley, Hugh, *Teachings of the Book of Mormon, vol. 1*, Deseret Book Company, 1993.
[10] 2 Nephi 27:13.

The Book of Mormon incorporates the *"words... concerning eternal life."* [11] It reveals the doctrines of salvation as bestowed by the Lord. It demonstrates the power of words to change hearts and lives. The words of the Book of Mormon invite all men to come unto Christ.

Ezra Taft Benson has emphasized that *"The Book of Mormon... was written for our day."* The ancient prophet Mormon, under the inspiration of God, abridged centuries of records, selecting what he determined would be of greatest value and use to us in our day and time. Hugh Nibley maintained that *"the matter in the Book of Mormon was selected, as we are often reminded, with scrupulous care and with particular readers in mind. For some reason, there has been chosen for our attention a story of how and why two previous civilizations on this continent were utterly destroyed."* Nibley believes that our world, *"is the world with which the Book of Mormon is primarily concerned."*

The Book of Mormon is prophecy intended explicitly and purposefully for our day and age. Moroni proclaimed: *"I speak unto you as if ye were present, and yet ye are not. But behold, Jesus Christ hath shown you unto me, and I know your doing."* [12]

---

[11] Enos 1:3.
[12] Mormon 8:35.

Essential

After reminding us of our critical need to study, ponder and apply the teachings of the Book of Mormon, President Monson counseled us that *"If you do not have a firm testimony of these things, do that which is necessary to obtain one. It is essential for you to have your own testimony in these difficult times, for the testimonies of others will carry you only so far."*

It is essential that we each have our own testimony. We are told that the Lord rains on the just and the unjust alike. While this is true, it is also true that the person who has plowed and prepared his field benefits most from the falling rainwaters. A witness of truth may fall on us as the rain falls from the skies but a personal testimony, a strong conviction of the truth of the gospel and the Book of Mormon, must be pursued before it is found. So, what specifically is required of us to obtain a testimony in these difficult times?

The beginning of all progress in any activity or endeavor is desire and desire must be the first step in obtaining a testimony of the Book of Mormon. Our desire to receive a special witness must be intense, unrelenting and persistent, otherwise we will not make the necessary effort or expenditure to obtain it. A testimony will only come to a person who sincerely desires it.

A sure witness and a compelling testimony, one that will endure the difficulties and frailties of a mortal existence in a time of devilish developments, will require help beyond our mortal understanding. Just as an astronomer uses a telescope to enlarge and expand his natural vision, it is essential that we recognize our physical limitations in seeking spiritual confirmations. A power beyond our own, the mighty power of prayer, must accompany our desire in our search for a strong testimony of Gospel truths.

With desire and prayer, we must follow President Monson's admonition to recognize the critical need we have to study and ponder the Book of Mormon. It is essential we make the effort to learn and understand the gospel of Jesus Christ and how it relates to our lives. We will devote hours a day to the study of science, or art, or our careers and yet, we expect we can understand the gospel and gain a testimony reading just a few verses a night. The gospel should be studied more intensely than any other subject.

Finally, the teachings and principles of the Book of Mormon must be woven into our day-to-day living. They must be tested and tried in real-life settings and situations. In the final analogy, that is the truest test of a sure testimony. The time will come when each one of us must know for ourselves, in our own daily lives, the value and importance of the gospel of Jesus Christ. An essential and enduring witness that will carry and sustain us through difficult times is ultimately the possession of the person who can stand on his or her own feet.

As Elder John A. Widtsoe confirms: *"A testimony of the truth of the gospel comes, then, from: (1) Desire, (2) Prayer, (3) Study, and (4) Practice."*

Vital

Not only did President Monson admonish us to obtain a testimony, he warned that we must strive to keep that testimony alive and vital. He continued his brief message with this caution: *"However, once obtained,"* explained the Prophet, *"a testimony needs to be kept vital and alive through continued obedience to the commandments of God and through daily prayer and scripture study."*

The secret of our church's growth, stability, and vitality lies in the testimony of each individual member who is faithful in the conviction that the gospel consists of correct principles. It is the very same testimony and witness that was given to the Apostle Peter. As David O. Mckay stated: *"This testimony is revealed to every sincere man and woman who conforms to the principles of the gospel of Jesus Christ, who obeys the ordinances, and who becomes entitled to receive, and does receive, the Holy Ghost to guide him."* [13]

President Gordon B. Hinckley also explained that *"the strength of this church is not in its buildings, in its chapels, in its offices, in its schools; it is not in its programs or its publications. They are important, but they are only a means to an end, and that end is the building of testimony—a conviction that will weather*

---

[13] McKay, David O., *Improvement Era*, February 1967., p. 2.

every storm and stand up to every crisis in the hearts and the lives of the membership." [14]

It is this testimony that must be kept vital and alive, as President Monson has counselled. Dilbert L. Stapley refers to a testimony as *"the strongest shield one can have against the fiery darts of the adversary."* [15]

The importance of maintaining a testimony that is vital and alive will enable us to pass through the dark valley of slander unscathed by the scorns of the world. *"If you have that testimony of truth on your side,"* explains President McKay, *"you can pass through the dark valley of slander, misrepresentation, and abuse, undaunted as though you wore a magic suit of mail, that no bullet could enter, no arrow could pierce. You can hold your head high, toss it fearlessly and defiantly, look every man calmly and unflinchingly in the eye, as though you rode, a victorious king returning at the head of your legions, with banners waving and lances glistening and bugles filling the air with music."* [16]

This restored Church of Jesus Christ is built on the individual testimonies of its members. No one joins the Church until he or she has acquired a personal assurance of its divine truth. The actual strength of the

[14] Hinckley, Gordon B., *Area Conference Report*, August 1971, Manchester, England, pp. 160, 161.

[15] Stapley, Dilbert L., *Brigham Young University Speeches of the Year*, May 23, 1971, p. 4.

[16] McKay, David O., *Conference Report*, April 1958, p. 130.

Church rests in the individual testimonies of its membership. We are small in numbers. Compared to the total population of the world, we are only a handful. But our testimony of the truth is our critical strength. We know that the Book of Mormon is true; we know it by the power of the Holy Ghost; and that is the actual tangible strength of this church.

"A testimony motivates us to action," explained Dilbert L. Stapley. *"It brings about a change in our hearts and lives. It instills and impels a desire to be an example and an inspiration to others. A testimony brings peace—a calm assurance—and it encourages us to conduct ourselves righteously and give kindly attentions to our loved ones and all of our Heavenly Father's children."* [17]

A testimony will inspire and motivate us to do the things that will bring us true joy and happiness. How magnificent it is when a vital and living testimony allows you to *"walk above the things of the world, and the weaknesses and wickedness of the world, so that you can look all men in the face and fear no man because you are walking in the ways of the Lord and keeping His commandments."* [18]

-----

[17] Stapley, Dilbert L., *Brigham Young University Speeches of the Year*, 23 Mar. 1971, p. 4.
[18] Richards, LeGrand, *Brigham Young University Speeches of the Year,* 10 May 1955, p. 5.

SPIRITUAL CPR

"When was the last time you read the Book of Mormon? Read it again. It will increase your faith."

- Neil L. Andersen

Do you remember when I asked you to imagine walking down a peaceful suburban street and unexpectedly finding a man lying prone and motionless on the ground? The first thing you did was check for vital signs, then, finding none, you began to administer CPR. Now I would like to ask you to check your own vital signs. I don't mean your physical vital signs. I'd like you to check your spiritual vital signs.

Is your testimony *"vital and alive"* as President Monson has stated it must be? If not, how will you revive it? I would like to suggest a little *spiritual* CPR that you can perform on yourself to keep your testimony vital and alive.

In his talk, President Monson reveals the key to maintaining a strong personal testimony of the gospel of Jesus Christ and of the Book of Mormon. The prophet declared: *"A testimony needs to be kept vital and alive through continued obedience to the commandments of God and through daily prayer and scripture study."*

Here is the secret to maintaining a lively commitment to the gospel of Jesus Christ and a vital testimony of the Book of Mormon. The three keys suggested by President Monson are:

Continued obedience to the commandments,

Pray daily, and

Read the scriptures.

This is the formula offered by the Lord's voice and servant for strengthening and maintaining our testimonies of revealed truth. This is spiritual CPR.

In a devotional address given at BYU's Campus Education Week, Elder Richard G. Scott expounded on these same foundational principles that will assist us in maintaining a vital testimony of *"the teachings of*

Jesus Christ, His gospel and the principles that flow from them."

Elder Scott explains that our happiness is guaranteed as we willingly obey the Lord's commandments. He encourages us to establish a set of guiding principles. *"With such standards,"* Elder Scott promises, *"you will not make the wrong decisions on the basis of the circumstances and the pressures of the day. Principles that you are determined to live by will keep you on track."*

The Nephites were promised that if they kept the commandments they would prosper in the land. The same promise pertains to us. Obedience to God's commandments is determined by our faith in Jesus Christ as our Savior and Redeemer. Our objective in obeying the commandments is influenced, in large measure, by our attitude toward the Savior. When we do not show gratitude by obeying the commandments we offend God and his wrath is kindled against us. [19]

A valuable source of comfort, direction and sustaining power is the gift of prayer. Elder Scott said: *"Too often in the routine of daily life, you may be tempted to offer hurried, mechanical communications to the Lord... Prayers that bring comfort, solace, direction and great inner strength are of the variety offered by Enos. His record teaches you the importance*

---

[19] D&C 59:21.

of praying 'with faith in Christ' and being diligent 'in keeping His commandments.'"

Elder Scott also encourages us to establish a foundation of reading and studying the scriptures. *"The scriptures"* he explains, *"are an excellent source of understanding and strength"* and *"fortify faith in truth."*

"There will ever be a need for you to walk to the edge of the light of knowledge and testimony you possess into the twilight area of faith," Elder Scott explained. *"You will be asked to exercise faith in truths you have not yet come to prove through your own experience or through the sacred witness of the Holy Ghost."*

A regular habit of conducting spiritual CPR, continued obedience to the commandments of God, daily prayer and scripture study, will strengthen your commitment to the gospel of Jesus Christ and help you maintain a testimony that is vital and alive.

"A knowledge of truth is of little value if it is not lived in full measure."

- Richard G. Scott

ANOTHER FASCINATING WORD

"If people are good only because they fear punishment, and hope for reward, then we are a sorry lot indeed."

- Albert Einstein

In his April 2017 Sunday morning General Conference address, President Monson used another word that struck me as powerful and compelling. It is the word *"implore."* Have you ever had to implore someone to do something? What makes this word so fascinating and influential?

One dictionary defines implore as to *"beg someone earnestly or desperately to do something."* Do you sense that to implore is much more powerful than simply to ask? You might ask your spouse to pass the salt or your children to turn off a video game, but when would you implore someone to do something? According to the definition above, it would be when you desperately and earnestly need something.

Think back to your imaginary interview with President Monson. Remember how he told you that it is critical that you study and ponder the Book of Mormon and apply its teachings in your life. Recall that he personally told you that it is essential that you have your own testimony and that it must be kept vital and alive. Now, imagine in that interview, President Monson leans forward in his chair and looks you straight in the eye. There is a depth of concern, almost a sadness there that you hadn't perceived before. You sense the trepidation in his voice as he speaks. *"I earnestly and desperately beg you... ,"* he says. Are you listening? Are you wondering what could possibly be so important that the Prophet of God would earnestly and desperately beg of you? He continues: *"I earnestly and desperately beg you to prayerfully study and ponder the Book of Mormon each day."*

Can you begin to sense that maybe this prophet really wants you to make a sincere and honest effort of daily studying the Book of Mormon? Do you imagine that you would leave that interview with a strong conviction to follow the prophet's direction and counsel?

As he closed his brief declaration to the world, President Thomas S. Monson stated, *"My dear associates in the work of the Lord, I implore each of us to prayerfully study and ponder the Book of Mormon each day."*

Implore is a powerful word, wouldn't you agree?

A PROPHET'S PROMISE

"The stars may fall, but God's promises will stand and be fulfilled."

- J. I. Packer

In the brief three minutes and eighteen seconds that Thomas S. Monson stood to address the members of the Church and the world at large, he imparted a message of great consequence and value. That message and counsel, I believe, is the will of the Lord, is the mind of the Lord, is the word of the Lord and is the voice of the Lord. [20]

Something I always seem to encounter is that when the Lord or His prophets give counsel to us, it is usually followed by a promise. President Monson's message and admonition is no exception. His brief message contained a powerful promise to those who heed his counsel. In fact, it contained four very specific promises.

"As we do so," stated the prophet, *"we will be in a position*

> *to hear the voice of the Spirit,*

> *to resist temptation,*

> *to overcome doubt and fear,*

> *and to receive heaven's help in our lives."*

We can reach greater heights and extended benefits when we maintain an eye single to the glory of God, obey the commandments and listen to the voice of the Spirit. To receive these spiritual concessions, we must lift our thoughts above the creature and focus on the Creator. The function of the gospel of Jesus Christ and the objective of revealed religion is to raise us to an exalted plain and position.

---

[20] See D&C 68:4.

Hear the Voice of the Spirit

The Holy Spirit identifies that which is true. The things of the Spirit can only be learned by revelation. God's voice is Spirit and mortals hear it as a voice in the wilderness. (It is *"in the wilderness"* because we do not see Him.) We hear the Spirit's voice stronger when we are persistent in our prayers. We should pray our way through this worldly wilderness daily seeking guidance and comfort in major events as well as minor occurrences. Some days we need to just check in and have a chat to let the Lord know how we're feeling and what's going on with us. We hear the Spirit clearer when we pray unceasingly.

"It is the Spirit which will bear record to your heart as you read the scriptures, as you hear the Lord's authorized servants, and as God speaks directly to your heart."

-   Henry B. Eyring

The Doctrine & Covenants depicts the voice of the Spirit as *"the still small voice, which whispereth through and pierceth all things, and often times it maketh my bones to quake."* [21] The voice of the Spirit whispers to us, it does not shout at us. As we learn to quiet our thoughts and listen within, we will recognize and appreciate this still, small voice because it will encourage us to act.

When you discern the voice of the Spirit you may feel impelled to get up and do something. Do not be surprised if you sense the motivation to perform an act of service or kindness for someone. God loves all His children. Your kindness to others means everything to Him.

---

[21] D&C 85:6.

Resist Temptation

Resistance to temptation comes from within us. It is an eternal principle that people cannot be made good through compulsory means. The path to strength and power will forever be a straight yet rocky and rigorous route while the comfortable, trouble-free trail often advances toward weakness and unhappiness. Resisting temptation will strengthen our mind and it will strengthen our soul.

"As a person studies the words of the Lord and obeys them, he or she draws closer to the Savior and obtains a greater desire to live a righteous life. The power to resist temptation increases and spiritual weaknesses are overcome. Spiritual wounds are healed."

- Elder Bateman

We are taught in scripture that, *"I can do all things through Christ which strengtheneth me."* [22] The Savior will impart his strength to us. His sustaining power and strength take over precisely where our resolve and willpower end. When we try our hardest and make our best effort, Christ will make up the difference. [23]

Living Christian values and ideals, following true doctrinal practices and obtaining a testimony of the restored Gospel make resistance to temptation possible. The greatest power that can come into our hearts and lives is the power of God. This power will give us all the required strength we need to overcome the adversary.

---

[22] Philippians 4:13.
[23] See 2 Corinthians 12:9.

Overcome Doubt and Fear

Fear is rampant throughout the earth. It restrains our resourcefulness, saps our strength, and lessens our effectiveness. Even more precariously, it diminishes our faith, creates doubt, and breeds distrust. Fear comes in all shapes and sizes and hampers the very substance of our existence. Experience teaches us that it is futile to be afraid.

"You gain strength, courage and confidence by every experience in which you really stop to look fear in the face."

- Eleanor Roosevelt

To Isaac, the son of Abraham, the Lord said: *"Fear not, for I am with thee."* [24] The declaration to *"fear not"* is distinct and direct and the subsequent promise, *"I am with thee,"* is powerful and precise. The same admonition and assurance is accessible to everyone.

---

[24] Genesis 26:24.

Consider how often the Lord has offered us assurance, comfort and encouragement:

Paul asks the rhetorical question: *"If God be for us, who can be (or prevail) against us?"* [25]

The Psalmist suggests that we should *"not fear what flesh can do."* [26]

Saul was rejected as king because he *"feared the people, and obeyed their voice."* [27]

The promise to the Israelites was that *"The Lord is with us: fear them not."* [28]

To Joseph Smith the Lord said, *"You should not have feared man more than God."* [29]

Freedom from fear is one of the four essential human freedoms listed by Franklin D. Roosevelt in a message delivered to Congress on January 6, 1941.

"Whosoever belongeth to my church need not fear."

- D & C 10:55

---

[25] Romans 8:31, JST Romans 8:31.
[26] Psalms 56:4.
[27] 1 Samuel 15:24.
[28] Numbers 14:9.
[29] D&C 3:7.

None of us need fear disapproval, disparagement, or discrimination in the cause of the Lord because we know and understand the outcome. The Lord's work will go forward. *"The works, and the designs, and the purposes of God cannot be frustrated, neither can they come to naught. Remember, remember that it is not the work of God that is frustrated, but the work of men."* [30]

We gain strength from knowing that the Lord is with us. To Abraham God declared, *"Fear not, Abram: I am thy shield."* [31] This is precisely what we need in this enticing, indulgent world—a shield to protect us from the *"fiery darts of the wicked."* [32]

---

[30] D&C 3:1,3.
[31] Genesis 15:1.
[32] D&C 27:17.

Receive Heaven's Help

We will all experience days when we wish things were better. Moroni referred to this as *"hope for a better world."* [33] Our spiritual strength (as well as our emotional health) looks forward to respite, renewal and hope. Sometimes it is enough just to know that there is the promise of good things to come.

We will all experience days when we will want to receive heaven's help, when we feel inadequate or not up to the task. Heaven's help is available! The Lord opens the heavens to his children. When difficult days come we can feel confident that he will provide answers and aid beyond our human understanding. Jesus *"is the mediator of a better covenant"* filled with *"better promises,"* and through His mediation and atonement, he became *"an high priest of good things to come."* [34]

The good works that really matter require the help of heaven. And the help of heaven requires working past the point of fatigue. Alma advised his son to *"never be weary of good works, but to be meek and lowly in heart; for such shall find rest to their souls."* [35] The Lord doesn't put us through this test just to give us a grade; he does it because the process will change us.

---

[33] Ether 12:4.
[34] Hebrews 8:6, 9:11.
[35] Alma 37:34.

"My help cometh from the Lord, which made heaven and earth."

- Psalms 121:2

The gospel of Jesus Christ offers us help, especially during our times of greatest need. There is help. There is hope. There is light at the end of the tunnel. It is the light of our Savior, the *"light that is endless, that can never be darkened"* [36] It is the Son of God Himself.

---

[36] Mosiah 16:9.

"The importance of having a firm and sure testimony of the Book of Mormon cannot be overstated."

- President Thomas S. Monson

THE POWER OF THE BOOK OF MORMON

THOMAS S. MONSON

APRIL 2017 GENERAL CONFERENCE

My dear brothers and sisters, I greet you most warmly as we are met again in a great general conference of The Church of Jesus Christ of Latter-day Saints. Before I begin my formal message today, I would like to announce five new temples which will be built in the following locations: Brasília, Brazil; greater Manila, Philippines area; Nairobi, Kenya; Pocatello, Idaho, USA; and Saratoga Springs, Utah, USA.

This morning I speak about the power of the Book of Mormon and the critical need we have as members of this Church to study, ponder, and apply its teachings in our lives. The importance of having a firm and sure testimony of the Book of Mormon cannot be overstated.

We live in a time of great trouble and wickedness. What will protect us from the sin and evil so prevalent in the world today? I maintain that a strong testimony of our Savior, Jesus Christ, and of His gospel will help see us through to safety. If you are not reading the Book of Mormon each day, please do so. If you will read it prayerfully and with a sincere desire to know the truth, the Holy Ghost will manifest its truth to you. If it is true—and I solemnly testify that it *is*—then Joseph Smith was a prophet who saw God the Father and His Son, Jesus Christ.

Because the Book of Mormon is true, The Church of Jesus Christ of Latter-day Saints is the Lord's Church on the earth, and the holy priesthood of God has been restored for the benefit and blessing of His children.

If you do not have a firm testimony of these things, do that which is necessary to obtain one. It is essential for you to have your own testimony in these difficult times, for the testimonies of others will carry you only so far. However, once obtained, a testimony needs to be kept vital and alive through continued obedience to the commandments of God and through daily prayer and scripture study.

My dear associates in the work of the Lord, I implore each of us to prayerfully study and ponder the Book of Mormon each day. As we do so, we will be in a position to hear the voice of the Spirit, to resist temptation, to overcome doubt and fear, and to receive heaven's help in our lives. I so testify with all my heart in the name of Jesus Christ, amen.

ABOUT THE AUTHOR

Bill Wylson is the author of over 30 published magazine articles dealing with family values, religious issues and religious education. His work has appeared in The Ensign, This People, Liberty Magazine, Success, and others. Bill graduated from the Columbia School of Broadcasting in Hollywood, CA as a commercial copywriter. He wrote trade journal ads for a major advertising agency in Los Angeles and public service announcements for a Los Angeles television station. He also wrote and produced corporate video presentations. Bill has written and edited policy and procedure manuals, company newsletters, brochures, employee handbooks, job descriptions, resumes, press releases, and public service announcements. He has also worked as a grant writer for various non-profit agencies, developing and implementing million-dollar programs supported by local, state and federal funds.

He has served as a volunteer Board Member of Advocates of Single Parent Youth, Special Fun Games for the Disabled, and on the Boards of Arts and Theater Councils. He has also served on Advisory Committees for the Volunteer Center of Los Angeles and on the United Way Government Affairs Committee. Bill served a full-time mission in Cordoba, Argentina. He has also taught Seminary classes, Gospel Doctrine classes, Elders' Quorums and High Priest Quorums. Bill has served in three Elders' Quorum presidencies, one High Priests' Group and two bishoprics.

Bill Wylson currently lives in Salt Lake City, Utah.

OTHER BOOKS BY BILL WYLSON

HIEROGLYPHS, GOLDEN PLATES AND TYPOS:

How "Corrections" in the Book of Mormon Prove Its Authenticity.

On the inside cover of his first leather-bound Book of Mormon my father had written the following quotation from the prophet Joseph Smith: "I told the brethren that the Book of Mormon was the most correct of any book on earth, and the keystone of our religion, and a man would get nearer to God by abiding by its precepts, than by any other book". Directly below this quote, my father had complied a list of scriptures which he had labeled: "Mistakes in the Book of Mormon".

Committing his writings to the future reader, Moroni candidly and apologetically acknowledged: "And if there be faults they be the faults of a man. But behold, we know no fault."

How then did my father have the boldness to make a list of mistakes in the Book of Mormon? To gain a better understanding of the corrections in the Book of Mormon and how they testify to its truthfulness and authenticity, we need to understand the process involved in making plates of ore and the method for inscribing on them.

Available on Amazon.com

SEVEN SUCCESS STRATEGIES

for Latter-day Saints

We all want to succeed in life. We want to enjoy good things and be successful in the highest meaning of the term. Given that life is everlasting, our earthly, temporal accomplishments have significance only as they affect our eternal success. *Seven Success Strategies for Latter-day Saints* examines our success in this life and in the life to come.

The principles presented in this book are based on the revealed word of God for obtaining eternal success, including material success, career success, wealth creation, successful relationships, true and lasting happiness, and more. --Discover your true potential. --Learn the secret to abundant living. --Uncover the key to all success. --Unlock the power of the Law of Attraction. --Learn how to achieve any goal. --Attain genuine success. --Give meaning and purpose to your existence.

Available on Amazon.com